Simon Stevens

The New Route of Commerce

By the Isthmus of Tehuantepec. A Paper Read Before the American

Geographical Society of New York, November 15, 1870

Simon Stevens

The New Route of Commerce
By the Isthmus of Tehuantepec. A Paper Read Before the American Geographical Society of New York, November 15, 1870

ISBN/EAN: 9783337140533

Printed in Europe, USA, Canada, Australia, Japan

Cover: Foto ©Suzi / pixelio.de

More available books at **www.hansebooks.com**

THE
NEW ROUTE OF COMMERCE
BY THE ISTHMUS OF
TEHUANTEPEC.

A PAPER READ BEFORE THE AMERICAN GEOGRAPHICAL

SOCIETY OF NEW YORK,

NOVEMBER 15, 1870.

BY SIMON STEVENS,

PRESIDENT OF THE TEHUANTEPEC

RAILWAY COMPANY.

TO WHICH IS APPENDED THE REPORT OF THE SPECIAL COMMISSION OF
ENGINEERS, APPOINTED TO EXAMINE THE PRINCIPAL ARTIFICIAL
WATER-WAYS OF EUROPE, WITH REFERENCE TO THE CON-
STRUCTION OF THE TEHUANTEPEC RAILWAY AND SHIP
CANAL, DEMONSTRATING THEIR PRACTICABILITY,
AND INDICATING THE PROBABLE DIMENSIONS
OF THE CANAL, ITS LOCATION, MODE
OF CONSTRUCTION, AND VALUE
TO COMMERCE

MADE

OCTOBER 16, 1871.

LONDON:
PRINTED AT THE CHISWICK PRESS.
1871.

INDEX.

THE AMERICAN GEOGRAPHICAL SOCIETY.

HON. CHARLES P. DALY, President,

IN THE Chair.

At the regular monthly meeting of the Society, held at its rooms in the Cooper Institute, New York, on Tuesday, Nov. 15, 1870, Mr. SIMON STEVENS, President of the Tehuantepec Railway Company, read the following paper on

THE NEW ROUTE OF COMMERCE BY THE ISTHMUS OF TEHUANTEPEC.

MR. PRESIDENT, LADIES AND GENTLEMEN,

THE history of the lines of commerce is the history of the world. The paths of trade, radiating from the centres of wealth and civilization, are and always have been the channels through which the mental and moral wealth of nations has been disseminated.

With the creation, deflection or interruption of main lines of traffic cities, and even nations, have arisen from poverty and weakness to wealth and power, or from power and wealth have descended into obscurity and ruin.

It is to some of these lessons taught us by history that we now ask your attention.

The East, the old homestead of the human family, the richest and most populous portion of the earth, has ever been considered the fountain of commerce. Its trade has from time immemorial stimulated the West, and enriched those communities which have participated in it.

Europe is of yesterday, and America of to-day,— but who shall count the wrinkles on the brow of Asia, or tell the wealth which her commerce has produced?

When we speak of the East, we mean India, China, Japan, and " the Isles of the Sea," with possibly a dreamy notion of Persia and Asia Minor. These indeed are the commercial Asia of to-day, but we have reason to believe that other empires as mighty, as busy with trade, and as brilliant as these, with great cities and productive provinces, have faded from sight. Those in Central and Western Asia were destroyed, not so much by conquering Attilas and Tamerlanes as by the interruption or changes of ancient lines of traffic. Pekin and Yeddo remain in the distant east, but where are Babylon, Nineveh, Tyre, Cairo, Thebes, and the countless cities whose ruins only remain as witnesses of their former existence?

If we may credit history, the mighty hand of war was laid upon them again and again, but the day of their final desolation did not come until the caravans of the east had found new depots and new lines of transit. Successive conquerors might lay waste Tyre, Sidon, and Damascus, but so long as the trade between the East and the West required them, they were sure to rise again with startling rapidity. Arbitrary power and the keen political sagacity of Alexander of Macedon, as early as the fourth century before Christ, diverted the trade of his Asiatic dominions through the Red Sea and the Nile to his newly-built city of Alexandria. The prosperity of that commercial emporium was so well established that to this day the dream of the Greek conqueror continues to be fulfilled.

In fact, it would be difficult to find a more complete illustration of the laws of trade to which we are directing attention than in the fluctuating fortunes of this Egyptian port, which seems now to have received a new impetus from the re-opening of the Suez Canal, which seems likely to restore to it much of its earlier prosperity.

The peculiar character of the commerce of the ancients and the character of the goods transported, at least for long distances, made it possible to conduct it, for the most part, by overland routes, while the sea was comparatively neglected. It is indeed probable that the canal, between the Red Sea and the Mediterranean, as it was originally planned under the Pharaohs, was but an effort to restore artificially a channel which nature herself had provided in an earlier period of the world. Whether or not the

Phœnicians under Pharaoh Necho, or the later Greeks, effected the circumnavigation of Africa, there was nothing in the ordinary commerce of that day to call for, or employ such a prolonged and perilous route, so, therefore, traffic adhered to its caravans and short voyages.   It will be gathered from this how very considerable must have been the commerce of those days between the countries bordering the Mediterranean and Eastern Asia, including the isles of the sea, to cause so many vast cities to spring up in the desert and flourish by the tariffs and tolls of a carrying trade.

At the beginning of the Christian era, all that was then known of Europe, Africa, and western Asia was ruled by, or was tributary to the Roman Empire. The subsequent growth of Christianity seemed to be, in a manner, circumscribed by its eastern limits. Centuries later, the Greek Emperors of Byzantium managed to revive and keep open the routes of Asiatic commerce, even after the fall of the western empire, chiefly because of the decadence of the commercial cities of Egypt.   The successive struggles and rebellions which desolated Asia Minor were but the efforts of mighty robbers to acquire the right and the power to levy tribute on the trade between the East and the West.

In the seventh century a power began to make itself felt in the earth, which, in at least its earlier career, was less a robber than a destroyer.   Its success operated not so much to transfer the ancient lines of commerce to new hands, as to monopolize

them altogether. The followers of Mahomet cared less for trade than **power,** their aim **being to esta-** blish the Koran **by the** sword. One **by** one the Christian **states** and cities of western Asia and northern Africa **went down** before the Moslems, and wherever **their** authority was extended all traffic **with the** Christian world **to** the westward was trans- **ferred** to their keeping, so that though goods passed with heavy tribute, all news from whence they came was cut off.

A description of the position of the commercial world about the time of the culmination **of the** Moslem power on its western borders, less than four hundred **years ago, has** been clearly stated **by a** recent writer substantially **in** the following words:—

According to Ptolemy, the best recognized autho- rity, whose geography **had** stood **the test of** 1300 years, the then known **world was a strip of** some seventy degrees wide, **mostly north of the** equator, **with Cadiz** on the west and farthest India, or Cathay, **on** the **east,** lying between the frozen and the burning **zones, both** supposed to be impassable by man. **The** inhabitants, **so far** as known in Europe, were Chris- tians and Mohammedans, **the** one sect about half **the** age of **the** other. Christendom, the elder **that once** held considerable portions of Asia and Africa, had been driven back inch by inch, in spite of the Cru- **sades,** even from the Holy Land, the place of its birth, up into the north-west corner **of E**urope; and, both in lands and people, was outnumbered six to one by the followers of Mahomet. For seven hundred

years the fairest provinces of Spain acknowledged
the sway of the Moors; and the Mediterranean, from
Jaffa to the Gates of Hercules, was under their
control. The Crescent was constantly encroaching
on the Cross, while Christendom, schismatic, dismayed,
demoralized, and disheartened, seemed almost incapable of further resistance.

The several routes of commerce to Asia beyond
the Ganges, via Venice and Genoa, by the Red,
Black, and Caspian seas, through Persia and Tartary,
were one by one closed to Christians.

The profits of the overland carrying trade, what
there was left of it, were mostly in the hands of the
Arabians; but Memphis, Thebes, and Cairo, which had
once flourished by that trade, had declined as it fell
off in amount, and yielded its poor remains to Alexandria, nearer the sea. Finally, in 1453, Constantinople, the Christian city of Constantine, fell into the
hands of the Turks, and with it the commerce of the
Black Sea and the Bosphorus, the last of the old
trading routes from the East to the West.

So far as Europe was concerned, Asia had almost
disappeared from the commercial world. From that
time forward the almost incessant wars between the
followers of the Crescent and the wearers of the
Cross rendered anything like commerce to the last
degree precarious and unsatisfactory, while the narrow and blinded policy of the Mohammedan poten-
tates almost prevented them from employing, even
for their own benefit, the splendid prizes which they
had won. Comparatively small as was the trade thus

permitted, and hampered as it was by perils, losses, and enormous cost, it was still sufficient to maintain for ages the splendours of Stamboul, and to continue for years the prosperity of Venice, Genoa, and other Italian trading towns. This trade, though Asiatic, was but to a small extent Oriental, in the true sense of the word. Though the silk and rich manufactures of China and Japan, and the "spices" of the Moluccas found their way to the remotest parts of the West, even to fair Albion, yet the consumers cared little to inquire whence they came beyond Venice or Genoa; for all beyond was shrouded in mystery.

Through all the darkness of the middle ages there were left some studious enquirers into the history of the past, and some sagacious prophets of the future, who were by no means ignorant of the great commercial causes which had from time to time built up and destroyed the old trading stations. Hence, the fall of Constantinople to the Christians of the West, especially those of Portugal and Spain, was but the signal of renewed energy to re-open the old paths of trade, or seek out new ones in order to secure direct participation in the fabled riches of the East.

The Spanish queen, whose steady heroism and religious enthusiasm sustained Spain in her long struggle against the Moors, was the same Isabella who, as soon as she could take breath after the fall of Grenada in 1492, sent for Columbus, her old suitor, almost as exhausted as were her own royal coffers, and said to him, "Now, sir, we will attend to you," offering to pledge her private jewels for his outfit.

Columbus was more than successful, and thus the same memorable year that gave to Mohamedanism its first check in Europe gave to Christendom a new world. There were many men at the battle of Lepanto who afterwards distinguished themselves as American discoverers and explorers.

The blind wrath of Moslem bigotry, and the oppressive exactions of Moorish avarice, operating as we have seen to close the old gateways of the East, were destined thus indirectly to promote the accomplishment of results whose magnitude it is difficult to comprehend. Truly the ways of God are past finding out. How often He rewards earnest discoverers with inventions they sought not! The Almighty who permitted the False Prophet to scourge a corrupt and debased Christendom, also permitted the nations who had fled before the Crescent, to find a new world while searching for the fabled East of the old.

The van of the new era of discovery seems to have been led by Portugal, whose peculiar position in the south-west corner of Europe, with the boldly projecting coast of Africa trending away south-westerly below her, must naturally have suggested the direction which her exploration should take. As early as 1454, the captains of Prince Henry of Portugal, surnamed "the Navigator," began this work in earnest, and by 1463 they had pushed their discoveries as far as Sierra Leone. That year, Gibraltar was captured by the Spaniards, and Prince Henry died. King Alphonso and King John pressed forward the work, so that by the year 1487, after nearly seventy

years blindly groping down the **coast of Africa,** Bartholomew Diaz had pushed southward through the tropics so **far as** the Cape of Good Hope, thus bursting **for ever** the barrier of ignorance and fear **which had sealed** the southern gateway of the Indian Ocean. **Still it** was another ten years before Vasco de **Gama** rounded that stormy cape **and** found **his way to** Calicut. The fact that this glorious **event** occurred just five years after Columbus had **success-**fully balanced his egg, **it** must be confessed some-what dimmed the splendour of its novelty.

A triumph truly these two routes **to the East, and** the beginning of **a new era** in commercial history; but Christians were **only a** short step in advance of their Moslem foes. **The** policy of Portugal and Spain was narrow **and** restrictive. What each dis-covered she **strove jealously to guard** for herself. The new Portuguese route **to Asia was** meant to be as confirmed a monopoly **as were** the old paths in **the iron** gripe of the Commanders of the Faithful. Spain **was not** more liberal.

But a new order **of** things was rapidly approach-ing. In 1453, **when the** Moslems captured Constan-tinople, and finally closed the **trade of** Asia to the merchants of **Christendom,** Columbus was a lad **of** six years at Genoa, Vespucci **of** two years at Florence, **and** John **Cabot** a youth **at** Genoa; but to these three Italian **boys** the world was yet to owe an immeasurable debt. While they were growing **up** in years **and** wisdom, the nations which were to **employ them** were also growing. While Columbus was slowly developing his convictions of the true shape of the earth and the true route to the Indias, Spain was grappling with the Moors in the closing scenes of that war of centuries, from which she emerged so gloriously. As victory enhanced the pride and ambition of the rising nation, the achievements of the neighbouring kingdom were looked upon with more and more of envious emulation, until at last, after long and wearisome waiting, Columbus obtained the scanty means wherewith to promote this rivalry of Portugal. The Pope, a native of Spain, wishing to reward his former sovereigns for their persistent struggle against the Moors, forgetting the promises of his predecessors to the kings of Portugal, and not remembering that there were other Christians outside the Peninsula endued with Christian greed and enterprise, divided the world between them, after the manner of a more ancient potentate, and fortified this monopoly by the boldest of papal Bulls.

You and I, standing where we do to-day, on the land which Columbus discovered, have by no means yet comprehended the full measure of his success, nor can we ever approximate to such a comprehension unless we place ourselves in the mental position of Columbus, and adopt as our own his dreams.

From first to last Columbus never so much as thought of discovering a New World. He did but plan a new route, whereby Europe might once more enjoy the wealth-giving commerce of Asia beyond the Ganges, and he died in the belief that he had indeed accomplished his purpose. For more than twenty years after his first triumphant voyage the Christian world shared in the belief of the great navigator. Henry VII. granted a license to the Cabots to open a north-west passage, and when they discovered Newfoundland and other islands, they took possession of them as outlying islands of China or Japan. The Anglo-Saxon race has not ceased to hunt for that north-west passage.

When in 1498, Columbus touched the shores of Venezuela he understood that the natives called the land " Paria," and he reasoned himself into the belief that this was the Paradise from which our first parents were driven. He and everybody else believed that these new lands and islands were in eastern Asia.

So thoroughly had the one idea taken possession of the minds of men that, for a century more, the coast of the Western Continent was explored by the adventurers of all nations, less for the riches itself might contain, than for that invaluable strait which should penetrate the mighty barrier and allow the trade of Europe to sail on westward to the golden land of commerce. We who assume the same controlling conception, as our peculiar legacy from our adventurous ancestors, will not be long in finding that it is of greater significance and brighter promise to us than it could be to the merchants of any European metropolis.

In 1513, Balboa first looked out from the mountains of Panama upon the waters of the Pacific, and in 1519 Magellan sailed through the perilous straits

which still bear his name, but it was a century later
(1619) before they rounded Cape Horn, in their passage onward to the true Spice Islands and the real
Orient. Meanwhile the persistent and daring pursuit
of this geographical *ignis fatuus* of a natural strait led
to a more thorough and practical acquaintance with
North and South America than would otherwise,
probably, have been obtained. Every bay and inlet
was explored. The St. Lawrence, the Hudson, De-
laware, Chesapeake, Mississippi, Goatzacoalcos, Atrato,
Amazon, Rio de la Plata, and other rivers were
ascended with varied experience of suffering and
adventure. Science profited greatly and the maps
grew and multiplied, but each consecutive effort to
penetrate the American Continent resulted in failure.
It is true that Cortez conceived the idea of a ship
canal from sea to sea at Tehuantepec, but the world
was not yet ripe for it.

For three centuries and a half the commerce of
Europe with Asia beyond the Ganges has toiled
around the Cape of Good Hope. The well-won
prestige of Portugal was wrested from her by the
Dutch, French, and English, who became involved
in a protracted and varying struggle which eventuated
in the all but undisputed predominance of Great
Britain in the commerce of the East. Lisbon rose
to commercial importance only to sink again, while
Antwerp, Amsterdam, Liverpool, and London attained
their wealth by the management of a trade which at
once reminds us of Tyre and the cities of Western
Asia and Egypt.

From the very first Spain assumed no share in the use of the African route ; for in 1493, within three months from the return of Columbus, Alexander VI. a Spaniard, a pope of not a year's standing, wishing to reward Ferdinand and Isabella for their struggles in expelling the Moors, divided our globe into two parts, by an imaginary line of demarcation passing from pole to pole, one hundred leagues west of the Azores and Cape Verd Islands, giving to Spain all she could discover within 180° to the west of it, leaving to Portugal all her African discoveries and the Indies for 180° east of it. After much dispute it was finally settled that the line should stand at three hundred and seventy leagues west of the Azores. Hence it will be seen how Portugal came to possess and settle the eastern part of Brazil, and why Spain confined her operations to countries west of the Line, and made no attempt to interfere with Portugal's African route or possessions.

It is now over three centuries and a half since the way around the Cape of Good Hope was discovered, and during all that time the trade of Europe with Central and Eastern Asia has steadily increased in volume and value. Every effort has been made to shorten the long voyages and add to their security : but until these later years the domains of the Sultan have presented the same impassable barriers that they did when Vasco de Gama made his voyage round Africa to India, while behind them lies what we may call the " dead lands " of Arabia, Persia,

Afghanistan, Beluchistan, and Turkestan, now receiving the fostering attention of Russia.

Not only was the trade increasing but vital changes were slowly taking place, especially within the present century, and the Asiatic question is not now what it was three hundred years ago.

English enterprise has secured to itself a vast eastern empire including the richest provinces of central and peninsular India. In Australia and the adjacent islands, a new Anglo-Saxon Commonwealth, more easterly than Cathay itself, is a new commerce springing up of vast extent. The lines of commerce are straight lines, seeking the shortest, quickest, and cheapest transits possible; hence San Francisco and Tehuantepec must eventually become the Tyre and the Alexandria of our age. America has indeed broken down the ancient barriers of the oldest empires of the world, and our future commerce with India, China and Japan bids fair to become extensive.

The great minds which direct the mercantile interests of Europe have never for a moment been blind to the dazzling future. The great commercial powers have been steadily aiming to grasp the prize. Russia has been pushing her conquests in the East up to the Chinese frontier, building long lines of railway stretching eastward, while year by year her trading fleets are increasing upon the Black Sea and the Caspian. England has increased her ocean steam services, shortened her lines of transit, built swifter vessels, and multiplied her Indian railways; while France, with a bolder and deeper insight into

the future needs of trade, has been negotiating
and toiling for the resurrection of one of the most
ancient routes of commerce, the canal, (once perhaps a natural strait,) across the narrow neck of
land which connects Asia with Africa, and separates
the Red Sea from the Mediterranean. Diminished
as is the value of the Suez route by the difficult
navigation of the Red Sea, the drifting sands of the
desert, and the gentle and variable winds of the
Mediterranean, there can be little doubt that so far
as Europe is concerned, her trade with the East has
entered upon a new era, which will probably ere
long work considerable change in the relative
positions of the commercial powers. One at least of
the paths which were shut by the Moslem conquerors
has been re-opened to the trade of the world, and it
is morally certain that others will follow in due
time.

The toiling caravans are to be replaced by the
rail and the steam-engine, while swift propellors will
penetrate the African Isthmus instead of the clumsy
barges of the Egyptians, or the triremes of the
Ptolemies, the Romans and the Caliphs, but only the
methods of transit will be changed, for there will in
all this be nothing new under the sun. Even if the
railway and the telegraph call into life new empires
and fresh marts of trade on the sites of the old
Babylons, Ninevehs, and Palmyras, all will but go
to confirm the primeval law of human commerce,
that "the trade of Asia is the wealth of nations."

We in America, heirs of the dream of Columbus,

have not only our peculiar interest in all this; we have a plain but most important lesson to learn, and we shall do well by ourselves if we learn it promptly.

When the failure of all efforts to penetrate the American Continent seemed to forever compel the commerce of Europe to reach Eastern Asia by the African route, the peculiar relations of the American continent to the commercial geography of the world seemed to have been altogether lost sight of. Not a hundred years ago, a learned society of France seriously debated the question whether on the whole the discovery of America had been of advantage to the world, that is probably to France. But now even though the nations of western Europe have found in the fast-expanding trade of America still another " Orient " from which to drain wealth for their capacious coffers, they seem to have utterly ignored or failed to comprehend the fact that America is, after all, not only a part of the world, but rapidly becoming the acknowledged central continent of it, and must hereafter hold the keys of commerce.

All these years, however, the New World has been steadily growing in population, wealth, and a correct understanding of its own interests, until now. At the end of these three and a half centuries, during which Europe has overlooked us, there has been developed here a commercial power overshadowing both coasts of the continent, and fully competent to take into its own control the guidance of the commercial future of this hemisphere.

The United States of America, are deeply interested in all movements aimed at the creation
of new, or the **deflection of** ancient lines of traffic
between Western Europe and Eastern Asia.

Let me **here** call your attention to a few considerations, drawn from the physical structure of the two
continents of North and South America. Some facts
are open to the most superficial observer. It is evident
that North America is not only very much the
larger, but that it lies wholly within that northern
hemisphere which contains the population, the history,
and the commerce **of** the globe. It lies, moreover,
almost altogether to the westward of South America.
The meridian **of** Washington almost escapes the
western coast **of** South America, while the meridian
of Cape Horn passes **to** the eastward of the United
States altogether. Tehuantepec is near **the** longi-
tude of Omaha. A **ship bound from New** York
to San Francisco is compelled, **in** rounding Brazil
and doubling Cape Horn to sail further eastward
than **the** entire direct distance between the two
cities.

Do not suppose for a moment that South America,
with her undeveloped wealth, is to have no share in
the western commercial system. Her position is such
as to vastly increase **her** commercial value and
intimate connection **with** both coasts of North
America, so soon **as our** own nation shall have
provided ample inter-oceanic communication. At
present the countries of three-fourths of the South
American coast are nearer, by steam or sail, to the

ports of Europe than to the Atlantic harbours of
the United States; nor are our Pacific ports better
situated in this respect.

When the slow and arduous task of ascertaining
the true nature of the geography of the Americas
was accomplished, and the fact was unwillingly
accepted that nature had left no break in the rugged
barrier which extended from the frozen sea of the
north to the Straits of Magellan, and even sooner, the
quick and fertile brains of the early navigators grasped
the conclusion that what nature had omitted must
be supplied by the ingenuity and courage of man.

The thought was promptly supplemented by deeds
of exploration so daring, so judicious, and so ex-
haustive, that if the records of their observations, now
at Madrid, should at this day be examined, we should
require but little additional information on the
American Canal question.   What Spain already
knew of the continental nature of the regions which
widened away to the north and south, though vague
and faulty, was sufficient to restrict her surveys to
the irregular reach of narrow land which extends
between Tehuantepec and Darien for more than
seventeen hundred miles.

At many different points in this isthmian extent,
enthusiastic explorers were positive of discovering an
eligible point for the construction of transits from
sea to sea, by ship-canal, or otherwise.   Even then,
the names of the Tehuantepec, Honduras, Nicaragua,
Panama, Darien, and Atrato routes, were as familiar
in the mouths of men as they are to-day.

There was then but one question to answer, and one problem to solve :—"What is best for Spain? and by which of these routes, if more than one is practicable, can Spain best carry on her commerce with the Indies?" The requirements of an American commercial system were not thought of.

So far as American interests are concerned, Europe of to-day is as regardless of them almost as were the Spanish explorers.

The reason of this neglect is obvious, when we consider that hitherto a route for a canal has been sought by or through Europeans, and the merits of each locality have been considered only with reference to European commercial interests, and the employment of their own capital. This, too, has permitted a species of political blindness, preventing them discerning that that route only, which was best for the trade which needed it most, could be most advantageous for all.

Let us once more turn to the map of North America.

At the centre of its southern projection, almost landlocked by the coasts of Cuba, Florida, Yucatan, and the mainland, the Gulf of Mexico, the Mediterranean of America, is situate precisely where it can best answer the demands of American commerce.

The great interior river navigation of North America has its outlet through the Mississippi into the gulf of Mexico; while a region larger and richer than all Europe, west of the Adriatic, is drained into its circling coastline. It is impossible to over-estimate the importance of this inland sea, and it would be something akin to insanity to dismiss it from consideration in connection with such a subject as the development of the American system of trade.

Let us draw a line north and south as nearly as possible through the centre of North America. We find that it cuts the southern terminus of the Gulf of Mexico, a little west of the peninsula of Yucatan, and at about the narrowest portion of the isthmus, which is on the meridian of the western border of the State of Missouri.

Here, and here only, can the trade of the Gulf of Mexico, and our swarming interior, together with that of the Atlantic and Pacific, as well as that of Asia and of Europe, be fully accommodated. If it be possible to construct at this point a railway and an available ship canal, nothing but the discovery of something approaching to a natural strait should carry us further to the southward, beyond Yucatan, or through the dangerous navigation of the Caribbean Sea. It should be borne in mind that the Isthmus of Tehuantepec is in latitude 18°, while that of Darien is but little more than 8°.

Nor should we for one moment lose sight of the solid truth that common carriers exist for the sake of trade, not trade for the sake of common carriers, and the end must in no case be sacrificed to the means.

In the determination of a question which involves interests of such magnitude as those which are now under discussion, no local jealousies, no minor con-

siderations of individual profit, or loss, can be enter-
tained. Nothing less dignified than the development of a continent or the aggrandisement of a nation
is entitled to a hearing. America will listen first
of all to the United States, believing, at the same
time, that the prosperity of the other political powers
as well as all Europe is bound up in her own.

In peace, which may be regarded as the normal
condition of our American national sisterhood, a ship
canal across the Isthmus of Tehuantepec would bring
the Gulf ports nearer the harbour of San Francisco, by
more than 2,500 miles, than would a similar work in
connection with the Atrato at Darien. A similar
advantage would be attained, in varied proportions,
governed by respective localities, for the Atlantic ports
of the United States, and the commercial cities of
western Europe. This continues true, in a greater
or less degree, whether we compare the Tehuantepec
with Darien, Nicaragua, Honduras, or any other
proposed line of inter-oceanic transit. The trade
lines from either coast of South America with either
coast of North America, and of the entire west coast
of our double continent with Europe, can be made to
converge more advantageously at this point than any
other. Nowhere else can all that vast preponderance
of the Asiatic trade, which is compelled by Pacific
calms, currents, and trade winds, to follow what is
called the northern passage, accomplish such a saving,
either in absolute distance, or in the specific facilities
of ocean navigation. The apparent gain which is presented by a superficial examination of the map is very

largely augmented when we take into account those
tropical calms and other phenomena which mark the
eccentric ocean that separates us from China and
Japan. If these truths are of such importance in their
general application, so much the more do they become
intensified when we consider them with reference to
that incalculable commerce which, in that event, would
converge towards and radiate from the shores of the
Gulf of Mexico. No more vivifying stimulus could
be given to the swift development of our southern
tier of States; no greater boon could be conferred
upon the valley of the Mississippi, than a direct connection by water with our Pacific coast and Asia, nor,
in these days of costly steam ships, should any need-
less day or mile be added to the time or distance of
their passage.

At the same time, selfishness itself forces upon us,
as a not unimportant consideration, that no stronger
stimulus to her commercial system, no better gua-
rantee of future prosperity, could be provided for
our sister republic. The statesmen of Mexico have
learned to look upon the Tehuantepec ship canal as
one of the bright stars of hope in their national
future.

It has been said that the history of the Suez Canal,
extending back as it does to the time of the Pharaohs,
Ptolemies, Roman Emperors and Moslem Caliphs is
a mine of archæological romance; but if that is true of
the Egyptian transit, it may be repeated with tenfold
verity concerning the central lands of America.
Geological observers assure us that the very summit

of the Isthmus of Tehuantepec is of coral **formation.**
The rocks that tower **above** these deeply **cut and**
winding passes, **were once low** islets, or submerged
beneath the bosom **of** the western sea, and at their
sunken bases **the** monsters of the deep played in and
out where we propose to construct our artificial channel. Speculation loses itself at once in **any attempt**
to imagine the precise configuration of **this part of**
the continent at that early date, or the nature of the
convulsions by which it was changed. We can hardly
guess if the mouth of **the** Mississippi was not then
hundreds of miles further to the north, **on the margin**
of a great inland sea, whose outlet may have **been at**
Tehuantepec, **and into the** western **ocean instead of**
the Atlantic.

The recent researches **of the Abbé** Brasseur de
Bourbourg have removed some **points of** Central
American Archæology from **the realm of** conjecture,
and placed them among **the established** facts of
science. Not only the Tehuantepec cliffs, but the
mountains of **the** Atlantic coast range, are of coral
formation. **The** most wonderful of our observations,
it **may be, and the most** interesting to Biblical
scholars, is **yet to come.** Who will hereafter sneer
at Noah's flood, when he learns that the mighty ruins
of Yucatan point so distinctly to precisely such a
general submergence ? These ruins, rivalling in interest, though perhaps not **in** extent those of Egypt,
are covered with hieroglyphical representations evi-
dencing a high degree of architectural and engineering
skill. What, indeed, shall we say, except that the

real history of the globe in which we live mocks at
that which has been written, and laughs at the feeble
light of what we are pleased to call "science." Well
may archæologists ask, which is the *old* world ?

Even so imperfect an allusion to the topography of
the isthmus leads us to observations tending to
correct a somewhat popular fallacy concerning the
Tehuantepec route. While much of it lies through a
virgin wilderness, and will encounter the obstacles
appertaining thereunto, that very wilderness is itself
a mine of wealth. Nowhere on the globe is there a
healthier or more equable climate, in spite of its
intertropical locality. Nowhere are there such bound-
less supplies of the most valuable woods known to
the arts and mechanical necessities. Pine, oak,
mahogany, logwood, lignum-vitæ, ebony, and other
valuable varieties of trees, are supplemented by the
rubber tree, medicinal plants, dye stuffs, and a soil
which produces in profuse abundance, coffee, indigo,
cacao, tobacco, sisal-hemp, bananas, oranges, and
endless tropical fruits. A large portion of this region
was under luxuriant cultivation by the hands of
white men, while yet the spot whereon we stand was
an unbroken wilderness. Here, on the banks of the
Tehuantepec, Cortez selected his own estates as
being the very garden of Mexico, and the surest
fortune for his descendants. Nor was he at all in
error. To this day his broad lands are held by
those who call him their direct ancestor, while even
Republicanism calls his estates "the Marquisanas."
Back among the hills and mountains lie towns

and villages, with churches that date back over three centuries, while hidden in the primeval forests are the majestic ruins of a yet more ancient civilization, older than the Spanish Conquest, older than the Aztec monarchy, older perhaps than Karnak or Thebes.

I have dwelt upon this feature of the isthmus country to better develop an important desideratum which cannot be so well supplied by any of the other routes proposed: to wit, the sure development of local population, wealth, trade, and agriculture upon these lines of interoceanic transit. Not alone would such a development create a local protectorate and guardian of the great work itself, but would rapidly provide sufficient resources of supplies, repairs, and other benefits to passing navigation, which could only be secured at great expense, and continual uncertainty in localities less favoured or more remote.

This region has at present no outlet—no regular communication with the outside world. Give it these. Give the people education, with toleration in religion, and you establish at once all the conditions of life, growth, and power.

Such, briefly, are some of the ascertained advantages of the Tehuantepec route in time of peace, and the most thorough and searching examination will but make them more strikingly manifest.

The history of the world compels us to assume war as one of the sure prophecies of all national future, and that misfortune will occur to some one or other of the commercial powers interested in the American interoceanic transit as certainly as the sun rises and sets. Let us hope that our own beloved land may not be involved, but only fatuity could allow us to lose sight of even that sad possibility.

In the event of war among any of the maritime powers, it will be of the first importance to all the rest, that so necessary a commercial highway should be kept sacred to the interests of peace, and not become, in the hands of weak or interested states, an object of warlike ambition or a scene of military operations.

Neither of these great ends could be assured should the proposed canal be located to the southward of the peninsula of Yucatan.

On the other hand, the land-locked character of the Gulf of Mexico, and the narrow and difficult navigation of its outlets on either side of the island of Cuba, would make this nation, conjointly with Mexico, the guardian and guarantor of a canal which opened upon the Gulf: and it would be difficult to over-estimate this advantage. We could not even approach a due conception of its importance without lifting the veil from our national future, and peering prophetically in among the eventful centuries yet to come.

In war, then, as in peace, the necessities of our commercial developments, the self-evident economies of trade, the dictates at once of broad statesmanship and prudent patriotism, point unmistakeably to the Isthmus of Tehuantepec as the best of all localities for the construction of our interoceanic ship canal.

We have assumed, what we fully believe to be true, that a canal at Tehuantepec would be of more value to the United States and to the world, than a similar canal at any other point to the South of it, and explorations have demonstrated the fact that at no point is it possible to make a thorough-cut from sea to sea. Such would be a preposterous undertaking in the way of mammoth cuts and tunnels, and would carry both cost and engineering into a region of dreamy and fanciful extravagance.

The Tehuantepec project, on the other hand, only presents difficulties precisely similar to those which have already been overcome with ease in other ship-canal undertakings in various parts of the world.

CHISWICK PRESS:—PRINTED BY WHITTINGHAM AND WILKINS,
TOOKS COURT, CHANCERY LANE.

REPORT

OF THE AMERICAN SCIENTIFIC COMMISSIO

ON THE ARTIFICIAL WATER-

WAYS OF EUROPE,

WITH SPECIAL REFERENCE TO THE TEHUANTEPEC

RAILWAY AND SHIP CANAL.

OCTOBER 16, 1871.

PRINTED AT THE CHISWICK PRESS.

1871.

COMMISSIONERS.

Brevet-Major-Gen. J. G. Barnard, U. S. Army.

Col. Julius W. Adams, Vice-President of the American
  Society of Civil Engineers; Engineer of Public
  Works, Brooklyn, N. York.

Col. J. J. Williams, Chief Engineer of the Tehuantepec Railway Company.

REPORT.

THE TEHUANTEPEC RAILWAY AND SHIP CANAL.

London, October 16th, 1871.

Simon Stevens, Efqre.,

Prefident of the Tehuantepec Railway Company,

New York,

Sir,

THE underfigned, appointed by you, a Commiffion to examine fome of the principal artificial waterways in Europe, with a view of applying the beft and moft recent experience to the project for an interoceanic Railway and Ship Canal acrofs the Ifthmus of Tehuantepec, Mexico, refpectfully report, that a portion of our number have examined perfonally the Caledonian Canal, the great Dutch Ship Canal now under conftruction for the purpofe of eftablifhing an eafy and direct communication between the port of Amfterdam and the German Ocean, and alfo the lefs known, though very interefting, work now in progrefs at the Hook of Holland, viz., the new Water-

c

way from Rotterdam to the Sea ("Waterweg van Rotterdam naar Zee").

The members of the Commiſſion have been courteouſly furniſhed with every facility for the examination of theſe intereſting works. The Lord Advocate of Scotland, one of Her Majeſty's Commiſſioners of the Caledonian Canal, kindly furniſhed us with letters to the officers in charge of the canal; the Superintendent of which, Mr. Davidſon, accompanied us, and explained the more intereſting parts of the works. To the eminent engineer, Mr. Hawkſhaw, and to his aſſociate at Amſterdam, Mr. J. Dirks, we are indebted for the fulleſt information, together with plans of the Amſterdam Ship Canal, one of the moſt remarkable works of engineering of the preſent day. Mr. Dirks perſonally accompanied us in our examinations. To Mr. Caland, the chief engineer, and a member of the "Waterſtaat" of Holland, we are alſo indebted for the opportunity of making ourſelves perſonally acquainted with the work at the Hook of Holland, as well as for documents and valuable information.

Want of time (owing to duties or engagements) has prevented perſonal viſits to other great waterways, eſpecially the Suez and Languedoc Canals, which would be inſtructive in reference to a project for any new Ship Canal; but theſe works are ſo thoroughly deſcribed, their characteriſtics and details ſo well known, as to enable us to diſpenſe with perſonal examinations. The various ſurveys and projects for Ship Canals at ſundry points acroſs the American Iſthmus, are of courſe familiar to, and have been attentively examined by us.

A brief memoir of the hiſtory of the railway and canal project for the Iſthmus of Tehuantepec will be in place here. This Iſthmus has always, ſince the early days of American diſcovery, attracted attention and explorations, as one of the moſt available points for interoceanic communication; but the project for a "Ship Canal" firſt aſſumed a definite form in the Report[1] by Señor Moro, founded on a ſurvey made in 1842.

This ſurvey originated in the conceſſion by the Mexican Government to Don Joſé de Garay of the right to open a communication between the Pacific and Atlantic Oceans, through the Iſthmus of Tehuantepec, coupled with the condition that the grantee "ſhall cauſe to be made at his own expenſe a ſurvey of the ground and direction which the route ſhould follow, and alſo of the ports which may be deemed moſt proper and commodious from their proximity."

Although the communication to be eſtabliſhed was not neceſſarily to be a ſhip canal, or even (wholly) a water communication, yet it is evident that ſuch a canal, or at leaſt a great canal, was contemplated both by the Mexican Government and the grantee ; and the engineer, Moro, expreſſly ſtates that to ſuch a communication his attention was chiefly directed in making his ſurvey.

In fulfilment of the obligation to make a ſurvey, Señor de Garay immediately diſpatched to the Iſthmus a Scientific Commiſſion, compoſed of Señor Gaetano Moro as chief, and Lt.-Col. de Trouplinière, and Capt. Gonzales of the ſtaff corps, and Lieut. Mauro Guido of the navy, as aſſiſtants, and Don Pedro de Garay, an officer of the Miniſtry of War, as ſecretary. The Commiſſion ſpent nine months upon the Iſthmus in the execution of its taſk. It fixed the poſition of the more remarkable points by aſtronomical obſervations or by triangulation, meaſured the moſt important altitudes by barometric or trigonometric obſervations, and explored in a general way the more important watercourſes and harbours ; and furniſhed, ſo far as it went, a tolerably accurate account of the Iſthmus in its geographical and topo-

---

[1] "An Account of the Iſthmus of Tehuantepec, with propoſals for eſtabliſhing a communication between the Atlantic and Pacific Oceans, baſed upon the Surveys and Reports of a ſcientific commiſſion appointed by Don Joſé de Garay. London, 1846."

graphical relations to the queſtion of a canal, and gave very valuable information concerning the mineral wealth, and the natural and agricultural productions.

Señor Moro baſed upon this ſurvey, a project for a canal of 20 feet in depth, and 50 miles in length, connecting the upper waters of the Goatzacoalcos, on the Gulf ſide, with the lagoons of the Pacific coaſt.   The ſummit was at Tarifa, at about 680 feet above the level of the ſea.

Further than to make the ſurvey mentioned, nothing was accompliſhed by Señor de Garay with regard to executing the canal.   After the acquiſition of California by the United States, this route acquired a new importance as a means of communication with our newly acquired Pacific territory.   Could poſſeſſion have been obtained at once, Tehuantepec would probably have become the eſtabliſhed route of communication, owing to the great ſaving of diſtance over Panama, as well as the ſalubrity of the climate.

Soon after the cloſe of the war between Mexico and the United States, the franchiſes and privileges of Señor de Garay, became the property of Mr. P. A. Hargous, of New York, who in connection with a company formed in New Orleans, aſſumed the rights and reſponſibilities of the Garay-grant.   But the neceſſary negotiations with the Mexican Government, and with other parties intereſted, delayed a commencement of operations till December, 1850, at which time the Company having applied to Preſident Taylor for an officer of engineers to direct the ſurvey, Brevet-Major J. G. Barnard, Captain of Engineers, was detailed for that purpoſe.   The aſpect of the problem was at this period peculiar, the great object being to eſtabliſh, at the earlieſt poſſible day, an available route for the great flood of travel between our Atlantic and Pacific coaſts.   Hence the idea of a canal was put aſide, and that of a railroad ſubſtituted. The ſurvey then ordered was therefore organized and executed ſolely in reference to a railway and a preliminary and auxiliary waggon road, and thefe it was urgent to eftablifh with the leaft poffible delay. Thefe facts not only fhaped the whole character of the furvey, but they even altered the route. It was neceffary to extend thefe roads at once to the Pacific (inftead of ftriking the lagoons, as the canal would do); and the " Ventofa," or " Salina Cruz," were the moft available points for the Pacific terminus.

Inftead of paffing over Moro's fummit (Tarifa), the more weftward paffes of Chivela and Mafahua were furveyed. Hence the furvey under Major Barnard not only did not coincide with Sr. Moro's at the fummit, but the entire route between the feas was quite different from that which a canal would occupy. The furvey thus executed may be faid to have been commenced in the end of December, 1850, and fubftantially terminated early in the following June (1851). Its refults are fo fully fet forth in the Report of the Survey, prepared by J. J. Williams, one of the underfigned, that we need only ftate that it eftablifhed the practicability of a railway route at moderate expenfe, and with grades not exceeding 60 feet per mile, and with a fummit about 800 feet above the level of the fea. The paffes furveyed were not fuppofed to be as low as the more eaftern one of Tarifa, and no obfervations whatever were made, fpecially directed to the practicability of a canal.

In the year 1857 the railway project was refumed, and a new furvey executed under the direction of W. H. Sidell, now Lieut.-Colonel of Infantry and Brevet Brigadier General, U. S. Army, a diftinguifhed civil and railway engineer, the object being a final location of the road. This latter furvey was made with much care and expenfe. Upon its refults and the previous furveys the line of location has been definitively laid down, the coft of conftruction eftimated, and everything eftablifhed necef-fary to the iffuing of fpecifications for contracts for the execution of the work.

Since the revival, under the impulfe of the fuccefsful execution of the Suez Canal, of interoceanic canal projects, the claims of the Isthmus of Tehuantepec for favourable consideration have gradually acquired a pre-eminence which was at first denied. The virtual failure of all the recent explorations instituted by the United States Government to find a practicable route where the isthmus is narrow,—as at Panama and Darien,—and the superior advantage of geographical position of Tehuantepec, its healthfulness, and its vast local resources for the construction of such a work, and its established practicability, in an engineering point of view, for a canal with locks, are now understood, and must have their weight.

In describing the different surveys that have been made, we have reserved mention of the most recent; and in reference to the establishment of the "practicability" which we have claimed for the canal project, the most important. We allude to the survey made during the last winter and spring by Captain R. W. Shufeldt, of the United States Navy, by order of the President of the United States, in pursuance of an Act of Congress for that purpose, and with the co-operation of the Mexican Government, for the special object of determining the question of an adequate water supply.

The final report had not been transmitted to the Navy Department at the date of our leaving the United States, but the authenticated copies of preliminary reports have been furnished you by the Hon. Secretary of the Navy, and are given in full in the Appendix of this Report.

We have in them, from the highest source and in the most positive form, the important conclusion "that an interoceanic canal of any necessary dimensions may be constructed across the Isthmus of Tehuantepec." We have also the further statement of the engineer on whose exploration Captain Shufeldt bases his own dictum (just quoted), "that a ship canal across the Isthmus of Tehuantepec is not only practicable, but also that the topography of the country presents no extraordinary obstacles to its construction."

The latter ſtatement that "the topography of the country preſents no extraordinary obſtacles to the conſtruction of a canal," is but a confirmation of the information obtained from Major Barnard's, Mr. Sidell's, and Señor Moro's ſurveys. The railway ſurveys and location paſſing over a line nowhere actually co-inciding with the probable line of location of a canal, does not of courſe furniſh the means of exhibiting a profile of ſuch a location; but moſt of the country through which it would lie has been traverſed by Major Barnard's, Mr. Sidell's, Mr. Williams' or Moro's parties. Moreover, it ſhould be borne in mind, unlike the country over which explorations have been recently carried acroſs the Darien Iſthmus, through wilderneſſes entirely unknown to civilized man, of which a ſingle line of ſurvey will furniſh but very meagre information, the Iſthmus of Tehuantepec has been a thoroughfare for centuries, while for the laſt thirty years ſur-veying parties have been, at intervals, traverſing it from ſhore to ſhore, either with inſtruments of preciſion in their hands, or ſub-jecting it to ſcientific reconnaiſſances. With theſe preliminary remarks, we will proceed to define the probable line of location for a canal, commencing at the ſummit.

The ſummit determined in 1842 by Señor Moro was near Tarifa. This ſelection was confirmed by incidental examination during Major Barnard's and Mr. Sidell's ſurveys,[1] and has now

---

[1] " As Principal Engineer of the Commiſſion under Major Barnard, while making explorations and a ſurvey for a railroad acroſs the Iſthmus in 1851, I took occaſion to examine the dividing ridge over which Moro had made his ſurveys for a ſhip canal in 1842; and although I did not paſs over the entire route as ſurveyed by Moro for a ſhip canal, ſtill I was at Tarifa, the ſummit, and on the moſt difficult ground over which he propoſed to conſtruct it, and I think I am ſafe in pronouncing the route, as ſurveyed by him, the moſt practicable of any yet explored."—*Report of J. J. Williams*, 1870.

It is alſo worthy of remark that in the Report of Major Barnard's ſurvey the " Rio del Corte " was indicated by the ſame engineer as a pro-bable ſource of adequate water ſupply for the ſummit level of a ſhip canal. See page 245 of his Report.

been once more confirmed by the furvey of Captain Shufeldt. This fummit level was barometrically determined by Señor Moro as being 680 feet (206 metres) above the level of the fea. The precife determinations of the elevation of the contiguous (railway) fummits of Mafahua and Chivela authorife the belief that the above ftatement of Moro is near the truth. The defcent towards the Pacific plains (elevated at the foot of the mountains about 240 feet above the fea) would be either by the " Portillo de Tarifa," or (penetrating the fmall " Cerro del Convento") by the valley of the Monetza to its junction with the Chicapa, and thence by the valley of the latter river. The latter route furnifhes the greater development (fay ten or fifteen miles) for reaching the plains. Either route is believed to offer no extraordinary difficulties, though doubtlefs this defcent is the moft formidable work of the project. No tunnel is neceffary, and the difficulties will lie in locating the bed and locks of a great canal along a defcending mountain pafs, in which the neceffary excavations muft be moftly in rock.

From Tarifa to the Portillo or to the Cerro del Convento, the diftance is about four miles, meafured over a plain fo level that in the rainy feafon it becomes inundated. To deprefs the fummit below the level of this plain would require a deep cutting extending feveral miles. Such a cutting, even to the depth of a hundred feet, in relation to the magnitude and importance of the work, of which it would form an inconfiderable part, would hardly be thought formidable ; and the refulting advantage of reducing the number of locks, and placing the fummit more conveniently in reference to its fupply of water, may quite probably demand it.

We fhall therefore affume that the canal fummit is not over 600 feet above the fea. The defcent to the plains at the foot of the mountains would therefore be about 360 feet, requiring thirty-fix locks of ten feet lift. From the foot of the mountains the canal, defcending through 240 feet with the natural flope of the plains, would reach the Upper Lagoon in a diftance of about fourteen or fifteen miles.

The main fource of **water** fupply of the fummit, as determined by the furvey of Captain Shufeldt, will be from the upper waters of the **Rio del** Corte, at a point fome twenty-five to thirty miles from Tarifa. The route of a feeder was carefully furveyed, with tranfit and level, by Mr. Fuertes, chief civil engineer under Captain Shufeldt, who found it entirely practicable. **Mr.** Fuertes finds the fupply furnifhed by the Rio del Corte, and other available fources, at its loweft ftage, to be 2,000 cubic feet per fecond, or 120,000 cubic feet per minute.

From the fummit towards **the** Gulf of Mexico, the canal would follow the well-defined **route of** the valley of the Tarifa and Chichihua rivers, to **the** junction of the latter with **the** Malatengo. Croffing the latter ftream, it would ftrike **the Goat**zacoalcos at **Old Mal** Pafo, which river it would crofs at that point.

The route from **Tarifa to the** Malatengo and Goatzacoalcos is thus defcribed by Señor Moro:—" This **part of the** country is the moft fertile and pleafant **that** it is poffible **to** imagine. Shortly after leaving Tarifa, it is truly interefting to obferve, **mixed together,** the fpruce and fir-tree of the cold climates, the oak of **the** more temperate, and the palm-tree of the warm regions. Further **on,** thefe trees, as well as beautiful green **meadows of vaft extent, occur** alternately, with woods of a luxuriant tropical vegetation. Trees of precious woods, wild cacáo, vanilla, &c., are everywhere feen. The plains near the rivers, cultivated by the inhabitants of El Barrio, Santa Maria Petapa, and San Juan Guichicovi, give an idea of the aftonifhing fertility of **the foil, fince the natives** only come in time to burn down the brufhwood, and fow without cultivation, fcarcely ever revifiting their cornfields until the harveft time."

Various confiderations caufed **the** left bank of the Goatzacoalcos **to be preferred** for the railway furveys; but there is no doubt that the proper location of the canal is on the right bank. A diminution of length by some forty miles, the avoidance of transverse ridges (easily surmounted by a railway), the fewer crossings of streams, and the avoiding of the overflows—all are considerations uniting in its favour.

From the Lagoons to the summit at Tarifa, and from that point to the crossing of the Goatzacoalcos, the line is so well defined as to leave but the mere details to be determined. From that point the canal, to avoid the great Suchil bend of the river to the westward, would follow, as near as practicable, its chord, crossing the Chicolote and the Chalchijapa, and approaching the Goatzacoalcos again near the source of the Coahuapa. This region is a dense forest. Observations taken from the summit of Mount Encantada, authorise the belief that it is unbroken by any great topographical irregularities. The only considerable streams to be crossed (this statement applies to the whole route) are the Malatengo, the Goatzacoalcos, the Chicolote, and the Chalchijapa. The second named is by far the largest. The ordinary rise and fall is seventeen or eighteen feet; but in exceptional seasons it is stated to have risen higher. The point of proposed crossing has been selected on a thorough knowledge of its favourable character.

From the Coahuapa to the junction and termination in the Goatzacoalcos River, the proposed route lies through a country nearly level.

The entire length of purely artificial canal thus approximately located, will be from about 115 to 120 miles. The number of locks would be 120 in all, assuming a summit of 600 feet, a lift of 10 feet, and also, as we have a right to do, that there will be no secondary summits.

We have now to speak of the harbours. The Goatzacoalcos, for thirty miles from the Gulf of Mexico, forms an excellent harbour. Its access is over a bar having thirteen feet at low water (according to the recent furvey of Captain Shufeldt).[1] This bar is unchanging, and we anticipate no ferious difficulties in attaining a navigable depth of twenty feet or upwards. From the bar up to the point where the canal (as we have defcribed its location) terminates, a diftance of about thirty miles, the river is generally over twenty feet deep. At a few points there are but fifteen or fixteen feet depth. Of courfe, to adapt this portion of the river to a fhip canal, will require channel improvements, and perhaps fome rectifications in its courfe—no work, however, of great magnitude.

On the Pacific, the Upper Lagoon furnifhes a bafin in which, in the region occupied by the iflands, and thence to the canal Santa Terefa, a depth of water of about twenty feet, with a mud and fhingle bottom is found.

To reach the ocean one or both of the narrow peninfulas, which feparate the lagoons from it, muft be cut through, and an external harbour, or entrance piers, thrown out fimilar to thofe now under conftruction at the North Sea terminus of the Amfterdam Canal. The works at Suez, thofe at Amfterdam, and thofe of a very different character at the mouth of the Maas, yet having much in common with them and with that which we are now propofing, are fufficient proof that, to modern engineering, the eftablifhing of a good entrance to thefe lagoons, for veffels of large draught, is quite practicable.

In the railway furveys it was important to reach the beft exifting port on the Pacific. Ventofa was firft felected. Neither this point nor Salina Cruz is confidered eligible for the canal, owing to the andvatages the lagoons offer for a capacious harbour, and the diminution in length of artificial canal and

---

[1] The furvey of Lieut. Leigh, **U. S.** Navy, in **1848,** gave 12½ feet *at extreme low water of Spring tides.* There has probably been flight if any change.

avoidance of river croſſings, but it is intereſting to know that there are already ſecure anchorages in the cloſe vicinity of our propoſed entrance to the canal.

The ſtatements given in the Appendix, pp. 21-22, ſhow that the formation of an external harbour on the Pacific coaſt, which will afford entrance to the Lagoons, is fraught with no probable difficulties, and that the coaſt is not a dangerous one, and that there now exiſt in the cloſe vicinity ſafe anchorages.

It would be quite premature to attempt an eſtimate for the work we indicate. Surveys of the line can alone determine the data upon which one can be made. But we ſtate with confidence that, for the length of the line and height of ſummit, it is rare to find a route ſo devoid of engineering difficulties. Moreover, the iſthmus furniſhes every variety of building material, while from its population, and that of the States of Oaxaca and Vera Cruz, can be drawn, at no expenſe for tranſportation, a hardy labouring force quite adequate to execute the work. The ſoil of the iſthmus and of the contiguous regions affords, in abundance, ſuſtenance for ſuch a force. The climate throughout is healthy even to European labourers. With a native force ſickneſs is not to be anticipated. Hence, ſome of the moſt formidable difficulties and ſources of expenditure in the conſtruction of interoceanic routes, at other more ſouthern points of the American iſthmus, are not encountered on the iſthmus of Tehuantepec. The coſt of earth and rock excavation or maſonry, ſhould not exceed, on the iſthmus, the coſt of ſimilar works in Europe.

In this connection we expreſs our hearty concurrence with the views of M. Thomé de Gamond, in his " Avant projet," for the Nicaragua Canal projected by M. Felix Belly. M. De Gamond ſays ;—" We think that after the example of the Dutch and the Americans, it is important to make extenſive uſe of timber inſtead of maſonry. The San Juan river traverſes a virgin foreſt, furniſhing trees of great dimenſions, both in diameter and height. Theſe timbers belong to the ' Conceſſion,' and can be employed in unlimited quantity, with no other expense than that of the carpenter's work. To overlook the value of these gratuitous resources, and to prefer masonry merely because masonry is more durable and more monumental, would be to increase expense for an empty satisfaction."

Again he says, " It would be an error to think that we can, in this enterprise, copy works executed in Europe under the formal rules of construction there adhered to. It is necessary, above all things, for the accomplishment of such an enterprise, to lay under contribution the immense local resources of nature, and to utilize in the employment of these resources that which is most applicable in the distinctive genius of every nation."

All that is said above by M. de Gamond applies perfectly to Tehuantepec. The immense forests of the most valuable and durable timbers which lie along the route should furnish the material for locks, bridges, and aqueducts, by which the expense of these otherwise most costly structures will be reduced to a fraction of that which masonry would require.

The use of timber in the United States for locks and aqueducts and bridges is so common that we need not refer to examples : to adopt its use at Tehuantepec is but to adopt the principle of M. de Gamond, and to apply the "distinctive genius" of American construction to an American work, and at the same time to "utilize" the immense constructive resources offered us in the forests of Tehuantepec.

In what precedes we have given no " dimensions" for the proposed canal. It would be premature in this report to do so. But it should be understood that we refer to a SHIP-CANAL with an available depth of not less than 20 feet, and locks of corresponding dimensions (say of 450 feet in length and 50 feet in breadth). The present transition state of ocean navigation, in which a substitution of steam for sails, and of steam vessels of enormous length for existing models, furnishes an independent and adequate motive for the use of timber for locks. While it would be imprudent to hamper navigation by " monumental " conſtructions of dimenſions which might prove inadequate to the future, it would certainly be premature to build, in maſonry, locks of the enormous length that ſome ſhipbuilders anticipate iron ſteamſhips are deſtined to attain.

We have but to add that the propoſed railway, owing to local reſources, and the extent of rich and productive countries which would become tributary to it, would command a lucrative traffic independent of interoceanic movements,[1] and would be almoſt an indiſpenſable auxiliary in the conſtruction of a canal, in which capacity alone it would pay for its own conſtruction.

We are, Sir,

Reſpectfully, your obedient Servants,

J. G. BARNARD,
Colonel of Engineers, Bvt. Major General, U. S. Army.

J. J. WILLIAMS,
Chief Engineer, Tehuantepec Railway Co.

JULIUS W. ADAMS,
Engineer Public Works, City of Brooklyn.

---

[1] See Appendix, page 22, Extracts from the Report of J. J. Williams, Chief Engineer, 1870.

APPENDIX.

CORRESPONDENCE.

Mr. Simon Stevens, President of the Tehuantepec Railway Company, to the President of the United States.

Office of the Tehuantepec Railway Company,
174, Chambers Street, New York.
July 29th, 1871.

To the President,

WHEREAS the Government of the United States lately sent an exploring expedition to the Isthmus of Tehuantepec to ascertain if a sufficient quantity of water exists upon the summit for the supply of an Interoceanic Ship Canal : and,

Whereas, the results of the investigation of that expedition, as well as the report of the Commissioners which co-operated with it on the part of the Mexican Government, are favourable to the construction of such a canal : and,

Whereas this Company has received from the Mexican Government its Decree, approved December 20th, 1870, authorising, in addition to its other privileges, the construction of a Ship or navigable Canal across the Isthmus of Tehuantepec : and,

Whereas the line of the Railway authorised to be constructed was duly located in July, 1870, but has now to be modified in order that it shall become an auxiliary to the canal :

Therefore this Company desires, before proceeding further in this great work, to obtain such information relative to the principal artificial water-ways in other countries, as may be beneficial in locating the canal across the Isthmus of Tehuantepec, defining the mode of its construction, and preparing plans and making the neceſſary eſtimates. With this view I have, as Preſident of the Company, reſolved to form a Commiſſion compoſed of eminent engineers, to whom will be referred theſe preliminary queſtions. Inaſmuch as this work is recogniſed to be of high National and International importance, it has ſeemed both proper and deſirable that an officer of high rank in the United States Engineers ſhould be on the Commiſſion.

I have, therefore, tendered the appointment to General J. G. Barnard, of the U. S. Engineers, and have named as his co-adjutors Col. Julius W. Adams, Vice-Preſident of the American Society of Civil Engineers, and Col. Lorenzo Perez Caſtro [1] of the Mexican Engineers, to compoſe the Commiſſion, to meet in London, as ſoon as convenient after the 20th of Auguſt, where I propoſe to join them with Col. J. J. Williams, Engineer in Chief of the Company.

I have the honour to requeſt that General Barnard may be detailed by the Hon. Secretary of War for this duty, and that he may receive the neceſſary orders to enable him to viſit ſuch places as the Commiſſion may deem requiſite.

I have the honour to be,

Sir,

Your obedient Servant,

(Signed)   SIMON STEVENS,
Preſident.

---

[1] Col. Caſtro having been elected a deputy to the Mexican Congreſs was unable to meet the Commiſſion in London. Col. J. J. Williams was appointed to take his place.

THE CHIEF OF ENGINEERS OF THE UNITED STATES IN REPLY TO MR. STEVENS' LETTER TO THE PRESIDENT OF THE UNITED STATES.

Office of the Chief of Engineers,
Washington, D. C. Aug. 3rd, 1871.

MR. SIMON STEVENS,

 President Tehuantepec Railway Co.,

  174, Chambers St., N. Y.

SIR,

IN reply to your communication to the President of the United States, asking for the services of Gen. J. G. Barnard upon a commission to meet in London, England, the latter part of August, 1871, to take into consideration certain questions connected with the Tehuantepec Railway and Ship Canal, I have the honour to enclose a copy of a communication addressed to the Hon. Secretary of War, with his authority endorsed thereon for Gen. Barnard to serve on that Commission.

  Very respectfully,

   Your obedient servant,

    (Signed) **A. A. HUMPHREYS,**

     Brig. Gen. and Chief of Engineers.

U. S. Navy Department,
August 3, 1871.

I HEREBY certify that the annexed are true copies from the files of the Department, viz : of Captain Shufeldt's letter to the Secretary of the Navy, dated April 18, 1871, and of the copy of E. A. Fuertes' letter to Captain Shufeldt, accompanying it, dated April 4, 1871.

   (Signed)   JNO. W. HOGG,

      Acting Chief Clerk.

BE it known, That John W. Hogg, whose name is signed to the above certificate, is now, and was at the time of so signing,

Acting Chief Clerk in the Navy Department, and that full faith and credit are due to all his official attestations as such.

In testimony whereof, I have hereunto subscribed my name, and caused the Seal of the Navy Department of the United States to be affixed, at the City of Washington, this Third day of August, in the year of our Lord One thousand eight hundred and seventy-one, and of the Independence of the United States the Ninety-Six.

(Signed)   GEO. M. ROBESON,
Secretary of the Navy.

Seal of Navy Dept.

CAPTAIN SHUFELDT'S PRELIMINARY REPORT TO THE SECRETARY OF THE NAVY.

U. S. S. Mayflower (4th rate).
Off Minatitlan, Mexico.
April 18th, 1871.

SIR,

TAKE advantage of the sailing of the "Kansas" for Key West, to forward to the Department copies of communications from Mr. E. A. Fuertes, Chief Civil Engineer, and Lieut. Commander Remey, in charge of parties in the interior. These reports show the results of the more recent labours of these gentlemen since my letter of 16th ult.

It is to me a source of great gratification to be able to say, that an interoceanic surface canal of any necessary dimensions may be constructed across this Isthmus. In arriving at this conclusion, I have guarded myself against considering the interests of individuals or companies, and avoided the partial opinions of previous explorers. Every inch of the ground has been gone over by my own people, and every observation carefully verified. The supply of water is taken from the Rio Corte, at a point never before visited or thought of for this purpose. The hydrographic surveys at the termini are entirely original. And in these three points the problem is involved. The satisfactory solution which we have reached as the result of much labour and anxiety, demonstrates the *practicability* of this important

work. I make no eſtimate of its coſt. It will be dear in point of money; cheap in point of American progreſs, peace, and proſperity.

Very reſpectfully,

Your obedient ſervant,

(ſig.)   R. W. SHUFELDT.

Captain Commanding Tehuantepec and
Nic. Sur. Expedition.

HON. GEO. M. ROBESON,
Secretary of the Navy,
Washington, D. C.

COPY OF THE REPORT OF MR. FUERTES, FORWARDED TO THE NAVY DEPARTMENT BY CAPT. SHUFELDT.

La Chivela, Mexico.
April 4th, **1871.**

CAPT. R. W. SHUFELDT, U.S.N.,

Commanding **U.S. Surveying Expedition to**
Tehuantepec, &c.

SIR,

HAVE the pleaſure **to report to** you officially, that a Ship Canal acroſs the Iſthmus of Tehuantepec, is not only practicable, but alſo **that the** topography of the country preſents no extraordinary obſtacles to its conſtruction. The junction of our tranſit and level lines was expected on the 31ſt of March, about one mile W. of the Cap-pac Brook. The datum **plane** aſſumed from barometric obſervations at the Corte, was **found** only eight (8) feet lower than given by the level. The ſummit level will **be** reached by a feeder about thirty (30) miles **in** length. **The** water will be **taken** at the river Corte, near the confluence **of the** Blanco **river,** and at right angles to the direction of **the former.** An inconſiderable cut through a very **narrow** ridge **dividing** the valleys of theſe rivers, will protect the feeder completely againſt damage by flood.

In addition **to the** Corte, the ſtreams Blanco, Majeo-Ponoc, Eſcolapa-Coyolapa, Pericon, and probably the Coquipoc, can alſo be brought to the ſummit level by the ſame feeder, yielding **a** volume of not leſs than two thouſand (2,000) cubic feet of water per second. This delivery is sufficient to supply a canal for the largest ships now built, and the excess of water can be used to irrigate and develope the agricultural wealth of the Pacific plains, now nearly sterile. The line of the feeder is nearly direct to the summit, through suitable soil, and presents less difficulties than the geographical condition of this part of the earth would lead to anticipate. In fact, there seems to be no necessity for accessory costly work, with the exception of a dam at the Corte, an aqueduct a few hundred feet in length spanning the Cap-pac, and the cut and accessory work at the outlet end of the feeder at the point where the Albrecias Cerro blends its eastern end with the Tarifa plains. Nothing remains now to be done but to establish by the level, the true height of the summit at Tarifa, which, thus far, has been assumed at six hundred and eighty (680) feet, upon the authority of Señor Moro's trigonometrical measurements. I intend to put three parties in the field, to level in sections, so as to finish this work in ten days. I shall start to-morrow for Tehuantepec, on a tour of inspection ; and, in the meantime, have written to the Mexican Commissioners, appointing an interview, in order to induce them to accompany me to Minatitlan.

Very respectfully,

(Signed) E. A. FUERTES,

Chief Civil Engineer.

THE SECRETARY OF THE NAVY TO MR. STEVENS.

Navy Department, Washington,
Aug. 8, 1871.

Sir,

YOUR letter of 5th inst. has been received. Captain R. W. Shufeldt at New Canaan Ct. has been authorized to allow General Barnard and Colonel Williams to examine the maps and notes of survey that have been or are being prepared under his direction to accompany his final report of the reſults of explorations of the Tehuantepec Expedition.

Very reſpectfully, &c.

(Signed) JAMES S. ALDEN,

For Secretary of the Navy.

SIMON STEVENS, ESQ.,
 Preſident Tehuantepec Railway Co.
 New York.

<div align="center">~~~~~~~~~~~~~~~~</div>

EXTERNAL HARBOUR, VENTOSA.

Extract from Traſtour's Report, **page** 108, *of Barnard's* **Survey**.

THE bay of La **Ventoſa is** much ſafer than the harbour of Vera Cruz. **Violent** tempeſts frequently render the **latter** inacceſſible during ſeveral days, and even when **the north** wind blows the communication between the town **and the** veſſels **in** the harbour is interrupted. During our ſojourn **at the** Iſthmus of Tehuantepec we have never had to record **one tempeſt** or hurricane **on the** Pacific Ocean."

Extract from Temple's Report, page 111, *Barnard's Survey,* 1851.

 . . . " From all the foregoing conſiderations, I am of opinion that **La Ventoſa is** not only the beſt but *the* point for a harbour on the Pacific **coaſt** of the Iſthmus. It is a far ſafer and better **port than either** Valparaiſo in Chili **or** Monterey in California ; ports in **conſtant uſe** the year throughout. I ſpeak from **per-** ſonal obſervation, **as** well **as** from an examination of the **ſeveral** charts, and **their ſimilarity** of outline has ſuggeſted the **com-** pariſon ; for although **the** indentation of the coaſt is poſſibly a little deeper **at** each **of theſe places** than at La Ventoſa, yet they are both open **to the northward,** and as **the** general 'trend' **of** the coaſt is nearly north **and** ſouth, **the** prevailing gales **blow** directly *along* ſhore, and *into* theſe harbours, creating a heavy ſwell, and often forcing **veſſels** to ' ſlip and go to ſea' for ſafety ; whereas, **at La Ventoſa, the** ' trend' of the coaſt is eaſt and weſt, ſo that the ' Northers' blow directly off ſhore, and create no ſwell whatever. The danger being from the *ſudden* ſtrain brought upon a cable by the ſurging of a veſſel in a ſea-way, and not from the ſteady ſtrain cauſed by the wind, it follows that northers may be diſregarded in an eſtimate of the ſafety of this anchorage, as was ſatisfactorily ſhown in the caſe of the 'Gold Hunter.' But northers, although frequent during the winter, and ſeldom occurring at other ſeaſons, are the only gales that blow in this region. The ſoutherly winds, character-iſtic of the ſummer and autumn, are ſaid to be nothing more than thunder-ſqualls of ſhort duration, and incapable of raiſing a ſea. Even the freſh and ſteady ſea-breezes that prevailed during the latter portion of our ſtay at La Ventoſa, were un-accompanied by any increaſe of ſwell."

Extract from Barnard's Report, page 117.

Steamer " Gold Hunter,"
Port Ventoſa, April 11, 1851.

MY DEAR SIR,

. . . "I am much pleaſed with this Port Ventoſa. The holding ground is excellent, and the depth of ſix and ſeven fathoms almoſt all over the bay very convenient. I ſee nothing wanting but a breakwater carried out ſome 500 or 600 yards from the outer point of the Moro Rock, to protect the landing from the ſurf, to make it an excellent port. During the four days we have been here we have had two of freſh ſoutherly winds, and two of ſtrong northers. The former did not agitate the ſea much, and the latter, though blowing very ſtrong, has not ſtraightened out the chains. We are ſtill riding by the bight which is buried in the clay bottom."

"T. T. MOTT."

To P. E. TRASTOUR, ESQ.,
Tehuantepec.

TEHUANTEPEC RAILWAY AND TRIBUTARIES.

*Extracts from the Report of J. J. Williams, upon the
Location of the Tehuantepec Railway and
Tributary Lines, 1870.*

LEAVING Minatitlan, the propoſed head of preſent ſhip navigation, twenty miles up the Goatzacoalcos River from the Gulf, the line takes the ſlope of the ridge north of that village and paſſes juſt ſouth of Coſuliacaque, thence juſt ſouth of Teſiſtepec, following, with but flight variation, and for the purpofe of correct alignment, the line of overflow, thence curving to the fouth and eaft of Lake Otiapa, thence curving foutherly to the eaftward of the hacienda of Almagro, thence nearly ftraight to within one mile weft of Mount Encantada, thence curving weftwardly and direct to the croffing of the Jaltepec River, about five miles weft of Suchil, known as Hargoufana. For this divifion of the road the line is quite direct, the curves of eafy radius, and the grades gentle.

The principle governing in this location being to preferve the grade from about three to five feet above the level of extreme overflow and at the foot of the flope of the high land which conftitutes the dividing ridge between the waters of the San Juan and Goatzacoalcos Rivers, and following this line, to preferve the fhorteft practicable route, to the croffing of the Jaltepec. At Hargoufana the Jaltepec is croffed at the level of 110 feet above high tide, at Ventofa. The line from thence fouth follows a depreffion in the ridge and rifes for one and one-half miles at the rate of fixty feet to the mile to the fummit, which divides the waters of the Jaltepec from thofe of the Jumuapa River. This fummit is juft fouth of the Picadura to Suchil, and is 290 feet above high tide at Ventofa.[1] The line thence running foutherly defcends for eight miles, croffing feveral branches of the Jumuapa until it reaches the latter at Pafo de la Puerta, with no grade exceeding fixty feet to the mile. Croffing the river at this place at a height of 155 feet above tide, the line then follows a branch of the Jumuapa, which lies in the direction of the route to the fummit between the valleys of the Jumuapa and the Sarabia, a diftance of fix miles, two miles of which is at the rate of fixty feet to the mile, with a total rife in that diftance of 195 feet. From this fummit the line continues direct to the Sarabia River, a diftance of four miles, over a gently undulating profile, and croffing the latter river at a height above tide of 305 feet, or a fall of but forty-feven feet in four miles, curves to the eaftward and following a branch of the Sarabia for two miles, with a rife of twenty feet per mile, reaches the fummit between the Sarabia and the Ma-latengo Rivers, at a height above tide of 340 feet, thence following a tributary of the Malatengo over a gently defcending grade, (Arroyo de los Venados, about two miles fouth of Boca del Monte), it croffes the latter river about 280 feet above tide, and near its junction with the Rio Almaloyo, and fkirting the bafe of the upland between the two rivers, takes the valley of

[1] When reference is made to high tide, it means high tide at Ventofa.

the Rio Almaloyo, which it follows to the plains of Chivela, a distance of twenty-four miles, rising in that distance 410 feet, or a mean rise of seventeen feet per mile, with no grade of over fifty feet per mile. Still following a branch of the Almaloyo, it crosses the Chivela plains and enters the Pass of Chivela at a height of 773 feet above tide, or a rise of eighty-three feet in four and one-half miles. This is the extreme height of the grade at the summit pass which divides the waters which flow into the Pacific from those which flow into the Atlantic. From the summit of the Pass of Chivela for a distance of three and one-half miles the line descends a tributary of the Rio Verde on a grade of 116 feet per mile to the crossing of the Guichilona, thence by the valley of the Rio Verde three and one-half miles, on grades not exceeding fifty-three feet per mile, to Rancho de la Martar, at the base of the mountains on the Pacific plains. This point is 240 feet above high tide at Ventosa. The total distance from Minatitlan to Salina Cruz by this location is 162$\frac{1}{2}$ miles, which is composed of sixty-two miles on the Atlantic plains, sixty-six miles through the mountain division, and thirty-four miles over the plains of the Pacific.

The maximum grade is sixty feet per mile excepting the grade through Chivela pass, which, ascending toward the Gulf, is 116 feet per mile, but only for a distance of three and one-half miles, and in operating the road an extra engine will be required to be used in assisting heavy northern bound trains over the summit. This should not be considered an unfavourable feature in the route from the fact that on one of the greatest thoroughfares in the United States—the Baltimore and Ohio—the same grade was adopted in crossing the Alleghanies for a distance of sixteen miles.

The maximum curvature is 7°, or a radius of 819 feet, and this is only used in the pass of Chivela.

In estimating the cost of the Tehuantepec Railway, I have before me the report of Major Barnard containing my original estimates, and also the reports of the Chiefs of parties under Mr. Sidell. With these I am able to make the following approximate estimate of the cost of construction :

Auxiliary and carriage-road between Minatitlan
   and the Jaltepec River $62,000.00
Auxiliary road from the Jaltepec to Salina Cruz   41,000.00
Clearing, grubbing, graduation, masonry, and
   bridging—Minatitlan to the Jaltepec . . . 1,200,000.00
Do. do. Jaltepec to Salina Cruz 4,120,000.00

Superſtruĉture—Minatitlan to Salina Cruz . . 1,271,922.28
Stations, buildings, and water fixtures . . . 216,000.00
Engines and cars 332,150.00
Engineering and contingencies, 10 per cent . . 720,000.00

Total coſt $7,963,072.28
Or ſay in round numbers $8,000,000.

This is the maximum coſt, but during the conſtruĉtion of the road, in working up the location, and in the modification of the grades, tangents and curves, for the minimum expenditure, it may be conſiderably reduced.

Article No. 23 of the general regulations governing the conſtruĉtion of all railroads in the Republic of Mexico, gives the Company the right to make ſuch changes in the line of location as they may deem proper and uſeful. It is very ſeldom that a railroad is conſtruĉted without ſome modification of the original location.

* * * * * * *

As your inſtruĉtions direĉted me to obtain as much additional information as poſſible, bearing on the ſubjeĉt of the railway acroſs the Iſthmus, I take occaſion to ſay that, notwithſtanding all that has been ſaid and written about Tehuantepec, I do not think that the Iſthmus has yet been fully deſcribed.

In the firſt place a map ſhould be made upon which can be laid down the coaſt and lateral railway lines which may be built to aĉt as feeders to the main trunk line, acroſs Tehuantepec; and in order to do this the plan ſhould include on the weſt as much of the States of Vera Cruz and Oaxaca as will take in the cities of the ſame names; on the eaſt, the States of Tabaſco, Chiapas, and a portion of Guatemala bordering on the Pacific; upon ſuch a map ſhould be projeĉted the following conneĉting or branch lines. Firſt, a road ſhould be conſtruĉted from Medelin, already conneĉted with Vera Cruz (twelve miles) by rail, to the harbour of Alvarado, a diſtance of about eighteen miles, over eaſy grades. Alvarado has one of the beſt harbours on the Gulf-coaſt and is about thirty miles from Vera Cruz.

The next ſhould commence at or near San Nicholas, a hacienda on the San Juan River, at the head of ſteamboat navigation, about forty miles by water above the beautiful city of Tlacotalpan, thence by the valley of the ſame river fifty miles to the town of Paſo San Juan, thence by the ſame valley thirty-five miles to Hargouſana, on the Jaltepec River, there joining the Tehuantepec Railway. This line would compriſe eighty-five miles of railway, and about feventy miles of inland navigation, and pafs by the doors of the cities of Alvarado and Tlacotalpan. A good line may alfo be continued from the valley of the San Juan over an eafy profile to Minatitlan, thus connecting the whole of the interior Atlantic flope of Mexico with its rich poffeffions on the Pacific coaft by way of the propofed railway acrofs the Ifthmus of Tehuantepec, paffing through one of the moft productive regions in Mexico. To give you an idea of a portion of this route, I mention that when on my way down the San Juan River in a canoe, I eftimated that about 100,000 head of cattle fubfifted in this valley; but on our arrival at Tlacotalpan, Mr. Schlefkie, one of the oldeft, wealthieft, and moft refpectable inhabitants of that place, informed me that I was entirely below the mark, and that there were at leaft 500,000 head in that and its connecting valleys. In the conftruction of the road this will be an important item.

The fecond branch railway fhould ftart from Rancho de la Martar, or from the point where the trunk line will enter the mountains from the Pacific plains, and run eafterly down the coaft, over nearly level ground, to the harbour of Tonala, and continue through that part of the State of Chiapas bordering on the Pacific, to the frontier of Guatemala.

Such a line as this would put the Tehuantepec Railway in direct communication with one of the richeft and moft beautiful countries on the Pacific coaft. I was informed by intelligent gentlemen on the Ifthmus, who live in Chiapas, that that State alone produces on the Pacific coaft annually about 5,000 bales of indigo, 5,000 bales of tobacco, 50,000 arobas of fugar, 5,000 bales of cacao, 15,000 bales india-rubber, 6,000 bales cotton, 6,000 facks of coffee, 50,000 hides, to fay nothing of the corn, ginger, vanilla, farfaparilla, and the immenfe amount of Brazil wood and other valuable products, all of which will be fent to market over the Tehuantepec Railway. The entire population and products of the Pacific flope, for fome two hundred miles eaft and weft of the Ifthmus, would find the fame outlet to market; and when the Vera Cruz and City of Mexico Railway is completed, would be placed in direct and eafy communication with the capital and the whole interior of the Republic.

The third lateral railway fhould ftart on the Pacific coaft, in the State of Oaxaca, at or near the outlet of the valley in which is fituated the city of the fame name, and run down to the harbour of Huatulco, thence to Salina Cruz, to connect with the Tehuantepec Railway.

This would place the filver mining regions of the State of

Oaxaca as well as the city, in eafy communication with the Gulf coaſt, and the city of Mexico, by way of the Iſthmus of Tehuantepec.

The great advantages of the propoſed tributary roads are their extreme feaſibility and the comparative eaſe and cheapneſs with which they can be conſtructed, the ground over which they would paſs, for the greater portion of the diſtance, being nearly level plains.

The above, together with what has been ſaid in Major Barnard's report, pages 139 to 142, ought to convince the moſt ſceptical that the *local buſineſs alone* would make the Tehuantepec Railway a paying inveſtment, to ſay nothing of the interoceanic traffic, from which a very large income may be expected with reaſonable certainty.

INTEROCEANIC MOVEMENTS.

Extract from the Report of J. J. Williams on the location of the Tehuantepec Railway and Ship Canal, 1870.

IT is only neceſſary to look at a map of the world to be convinced of the immenſe relative advantages in poſition, above all others, which a ſhip canal acroſs the Iſthmus of Tehuantepec would offer to the commerce of the world, and more eſpecially to that of the United States.

By this route the products of the valley of the Miſſiſſippi may be ſhipped from the gulf ports direct for China, Japan, weſt coaſt of North and South America, and the iſlands of the Pacific ; and the imports from thoſe countries may be brought home to the ports of Texas, New Orleans, Mobile, Penſacola, and from thence tranſhipped to Memphis, Cairo, St. Louis, Louiſville, and Cincinnati, and be diſtributed throughout the Southern and Weſtern States, even to the frontier of Britiſh America, at one-third the coſt of tranſportation of the ſame articles by the Pacific Railroad. In a word, the completion of the Ship Canal acroſs Tehuantepec will not only open a direct outlet from the Gulf of Mexico and the Atlantic to India and China, but alſo from the Miſſiſſippi River and tributaries, whereby the ſea-going veſſels plying upon thoſe waters will be able to proceed with ſafety to any port on the Pacific. Thus giving to St. Louis, the Queen city of the Weſt, and the whole valley of the Miſſiſſippi, direct water communication with the Pacific ſide of North, Central, and South America. In a word, the completion of the Tehuantepec Ship Canal would be the opening of the mouth of the Miſſiſſippi River into the Pacific Ocean—another world of waters.

The Iſthmus belongs, in its greateſt part, to the State of Oaxaca, which has a population of 600,000, and the reſt to the State of Vera Cruz, which has 300,000, and is bounded on the eaſt by the State of Chiapas, which has 200,000. In theſe three States alone, from 8,000 to 10,000 good and hardy acclimated labourers, ſuperior in ſtrength and morality to the Chineſe, can be had for leſs than fifty cents per day of twelve hours, and they board themſelves; and beſides from theſe ſources, labour, to any extent that can be utiliſed, may be had from Tabaſco and other parts of Mexico. This great enterpriſe itſelf would give work to thouſands of the ſons of that Republic, now without employment, and therefore reſtleſs.

The following ſtatement, condenſed from official tables, ſhows the ſaving to the trade of the world, in inſurance on veſſels and cargoes, profits on time ſaved, intereſt on cargoes, ſaving of wear and tear of ſhips, ſaving of wages, proviſions, &c., by uſing the Tehuantepec Canal.

United States . . .	$35,995,930.00
England . . .	9,950,348.00
France	2,183,930.00
Other countries . . .	1,400,000.00
Total yearly ſaving . .	$49,530,208.00

If the trade increaſes annually ten per cent., or one hundred per cent. in the next decade, the ſaving to the world will then be double the above amount.

As the annual increaſe of the trade of Great Britain, France, and the United States, is, together, more than ten per cent., the ſaving to the maritime powers of the world of 49,530,208.00 dollars in one year, at the end of ten years will be 99,060,416 dollars.[1] Aſſuming the trade only of the three powers to increaſe in the ſame proportion, the aggregate total amount ſaved at the end of ten years, will be over ſeven hundred millions of dollars.

[1] See Report of S. J. Abert, C.E., entitled "Is a ſhip canal practicable?"

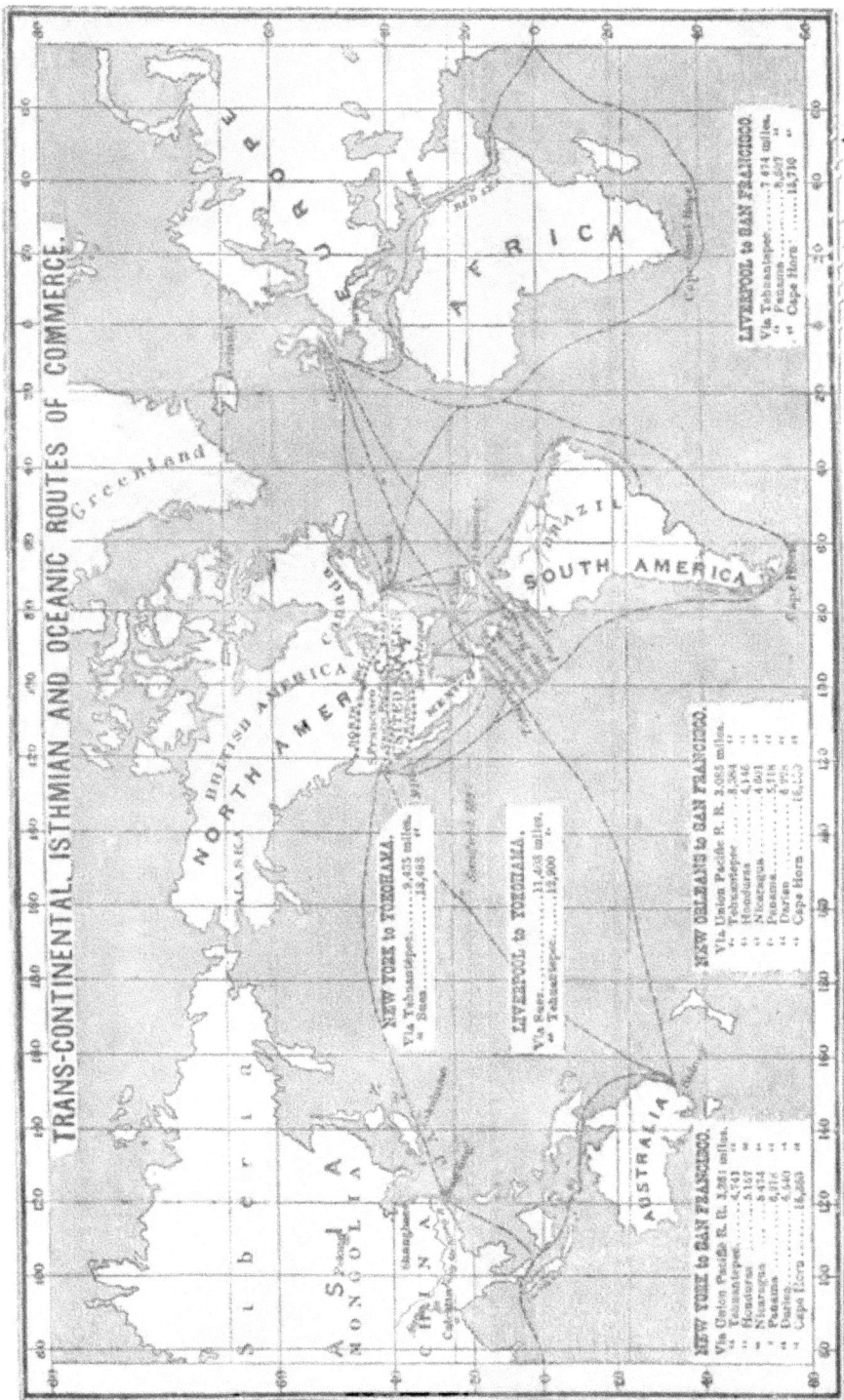

TRANS-CONTINENTAL ISTHMIAN AND OCEANIC ROUTES OF COMMERCE.

LIVERPOOL to SAN FRANCISCO.
Via Tehuantepec............7,474 miles.
"   Panama..................8,507 "
"   Cape Horn..............14,710 "

NEW YORK to YOKOHAMA.
Via Tehuantepec.........9,435 miles.
"   Suez.................13,483 "

LIVERPOOL to YOKOHAMA.
Via Suez................11,408 miles.
"   Tehuantepec.........13,003 "

NEW ORLEANS to SAN FRANCISCO.
Via Union Pacific R. R. 3,085 miles.
"   Tehuantepec.........3,304 "
"   Honduras............4,146 "
"   Nicaragua...........4,601 "
"   Panama..............5,118 "
"   Darien..............5,795 "
"   Cape Horn..........16,500 "

NEW YORK to SAN FRANCISCO.
Via Union Pacific R. R. 3,281 miles.
"   Tehuantepec.........4,741 "
"   Honduras............5,157 "
"   Nicaragua...........5,474 "
"   Panama..............6,010 "
"   Darien..............6,540 "
"   Cape Horn..........15,660 "

Suppofe the average tonnage of fhips to be 1,000 tons each, then, as per the tables in this report, 3,049 fhips would be requifite to carry the freight which would now annually feek the Ifthmus route. Abert, eftimating for Darien or Panama, makes the annual faving for each fhip 15,420.00 dollars, giving as the aggregate faved upon the tonnage which would pafs the Ifthmus the fum of 47,709,480 dollars ; and the faving of one year, at the end of ten years, would be 95,418,960 dollars, fums fufficiently near the firft to eftablifh their correctnefs.

Again, by a comparifon of time and money, in the paffage of a 1,000 ton fhip from New York to California viâ Cape Horn, with what it would be by way of Tehuantepec, it is eftimated[1] that the faving on the fhip and cargo would be 13,300 dollars, or 13.30 dollars per ton, againft a toll not to exceed 2.50 per ton. Allowing the fhip to make but four trips per annum of forty-five days each, via the canal, it would give a yearly faving of 53,200 dollars. Deducting 10,000 dollars, the toll on the four trips, there refults a net annual faving on a fingle one thoufand tons fhip, of 43,200 dollars.

Whale fhips and coafting veffels have been eftimated generally at forty dollars per ton. The United States and European commerce around the capes, is conducted in firft-clafs fhips, which often coft eighty dollars per ton. Fifty dollars has therefore been taken as a fair average value, in the conftruction of thefe tables, which do not include coafting trade nor the trade of any of the powers of the world, except England, France, and the United States.

The following tables fhow the trade of the United States, England, and France, which would probably pafs through the Ifthmus Canal if now finifhed, taken from the official returns of 1857 and 1858.

TRADE OF THE UNITED STATES which muft pafs through the canal.

Countries traded with.	Tonnage.	Exports and Imports.
Alafka	5,735 .	$126,537
Dutch Eaft Indies . . .	16,589 .	904,550
Britifh Auftralia and N. Zealand .	52,105 .	4,728,083
Britifh Eaft Indies . . .	177,121 .	11,744,151

---

[1] **Vide** " Engineering," London, Vol. V., firft half yearly.

French Eaſt Indies . . .	3,665 .	98,432
Half of Mexico	34,673 .	9,601,063
Half of New Granada . .	131,708 .	5,375,354
Central America . . .	36,599 .	425,081
Chili	63,749 .	6,645,634
Peru	193,131 .	716,679
Ecuador	1,979 .	48,979
Sandwich Iſlands . . .	33,876 .	1,157,849
China	123,578 .	12,752,062
Other Ports in Aſia and Pacific .	4,549 .	80,143
Whale Fiſheries . . .	116,730 .	10,796,090
California to Eaſt United States .	861,698 .	35,000,000

Value of cargoes . . .	. .	$100,294,687
Total tonnage	1,857,485	
Value of ſhips at $50 per ton	. .	92,874,250
Total value of ſhips and cargoes .	. .	$193,168,937

TRADE OF FRANCE which would paſs through the Canal.

Countries traded with.		Tonnage.	Exports and Imports.
Chili		25,688	$10,000,000
Peru		35,096 .	13,160,000
Half of Mexico		10,004 .	2,790,000
Half of New Granada . . .		2,389 .	1,090,000
Ecuador		1,650 .	440,000
Bolivia		1,000 .	100,000
California		8,997 .	2,073,859
China . } Outward only {		2,028 .	2,180,000
Dutch Eaſt Indies }		20,400 .	4,440,000
Sandwich Iſlands . . .		4,119 .	2,000,000
Philippine Iſlands . . .		1,463 .	1,000,000
Auſtralia		50,000 .	19,800,000

Value of cargoes . . .		.	. $59,073,859
Total tonnage		162,735	
Value of ſhips at $50 per ton		. .	8,136,750
Total value of ſhips and cargoes .		. .	$67,210,609

TRADE OF ENGLAND which would pafs through the Canal.

Countries traded with.	Tonnage.	Exports and Imports.
Half of Mexico	11,833 .	$2,775,137
Half of Central America . .	5,615 .	1,244,817
Half of New Granada .	10,188 .	2,437,605
Chili	118,311 .	15,486,110
Peru	244,319 .	20,473,520
Ecuador	1,820 .	360,015
China ⎫ . ⎧	16,853 .	7,077,390
Java ⎬ Outward only ⎨	16,003 .	3,821,410
Singapore ⎭ . ⎩	16,500 .	4,364,070
Auftralia	522,426 .	78,246,095
Sandwich Iflands . . .	1,950 .	520,560
California	11,800 .	2,378,105

Value of cargoes . . .		$139,184,834
Total tonnage . . .	1,029,295	
Value of fhips at $50 per ton .		51,464,750
Total value of fhips and cargoes . .		$190,649,584

The value of the tonnage which would take the Tehuantepec route is, according to the above tables :

United States	$92,874,250
England	51,464,750
France	8,136,750
	$152,475,750

TOTAL VALUE OF EXPORTS AND IMPORTS taking the fame route is :

United States . . .	$193,168,937.00
England . . .	190,649,584.00
France	67,210,609.00
Total value of trade of the three Powers paffing the Ifthmus . .	$451,029,132.00

E

Estimated Tonnage to paſs through the canal :

United States	1,857,485
England	1,029,295
France	162,735
Total tonnage	3,049,515

Upon the above tonnage, the yearly income, at two dollars per ton, would be £6,099,030, which is the eſtimated annual groſs receipts from tolls upon ſhips belonging to the United States, England, and France.

This calculation does not include the United States' coaſting trade on both oceans, nor the trade that might be expected from the other nations of the world not mentioned.

The amount of 2,500 dollars toll, now charged on a ſhip of 1,000 tons on the Suez Canal, would increaſe the above eſtimated yearly income on Tehuantepec, to 7,625,000 dollars. This amount, baſed upon the yearly ten per cent. increaſe would double itſelf in ten years.

In 1860, the maritime movement between Europe and the Eaſt, by way of the Cape of Good Hope, amounted to 7,250,000 tons. The aſcertained rate of progreſs would give for 1870 a total of 11,000,000 tons, one half of which, at leaſt, would paſs through the Suez Canal, and poſſibly a fifth by way of the American Iſthmus.

Taking theſe facts into conſideration, and bearing in mind that none of the trade of the Weſtern Hemiſphere is included in the 11,000,000 tons, it remains for commercial men to ſay whether or not we are correct in eſtimating an annual amount of 3,000,000 tons as likely to paſs through the American Iſthmus.

I have the honour to be, very reſpectfully,

Your obedient ſervant,

J. J. Williams,

Chief Engineer Tehuantepec Railway Co.

CHISWICK PRESS:—PRINTED BY WHITTINGHAM AND WILKINS, TOOKS COURT, CHANCERY LANE, LONDON.

www.ingramcontent.com/pod-product-compliance
Lightning Source LLC
Chambersburg PA
CBHW021628270326
41931CB00008B/926